The book is beautifully illustrated and carries a simple and extremely powerful story . . pitched just right for young children to engage with on a number of different levels. It would be useful to all children, regardless of whether they themselves are experiencing coercive control. The resources that accompany it are absolutely excellent for supporting professionals to use the book with children.

With its vitally important message and engaging story, *Floss and the Boss* is an essential resource.

Dr Emma Katz, Ph.D.
Senior Lecturer in Childhood and Youth,
Liverpool Hope University, UK

Helping Children Learn About Domestic Abuse and Coercive Control

This book is designed to support professionals with the sensitive and effective use of the storybook, *Floss and the Boss*, created to help young children understand about domestic abuse and coercive control.

By defining domestic abuse and coercive control and exploring the effects upon children and their education, this guidebook puts the professional in a position to have important conversations with children about what to do if something at home does not feel right. When used with the storybook, it provides a vehicle for talking to children about staying safe and their emotional wellbeing.

Key features of this book include:

- Page-by-page notes, with discussion topics and points for conversation around the *Floss and the Boss* story
- Activities for supporting children, safety planning strategies and guidance for taking on a key adult role
- A comprehensive list of helplines and organisations in place to support adult victims of domestic abuse

This is a vital tool for teachers, social care staff, therapists and other professionals working with the *Floss and the Boss* story to teach young children about domestic abuse and coercive control.

Catherine Lawler works as a training consultant for a Safeguarding Children's Partnership. She has extensive experience of working with children, young people and families. She has worked as a children's therapist, specialising in domestic abuse. She has developed resources on bullying, peer-on-peer abuse and children accessing sexualised imagery.

Abigail Sterne is a senior educational psychologist working in schools in Manchester and is a former teacher. She works closely with Central Manchester Child and Adolescent Mental Health Services (CAMHS) and has worked with fostering and adoption services.

Catherine and Abigail are co-authors of *Domestic Violence and Children: A Handbook for Schools and Early Years Settings* (Routledge, 2010). They have developed domestic abuse and safeguarding training packages for education and social care services. They wrote and delivered initial training for key adults for Operation Encompass, whereby key trained adults in schools receive prompt police notifications about abusive incidents. For this they received Commander's Certificates from Devon and Cornwall Constabulary.

Nicky Armstrong, B.A.(Hons) Theatre Design, M.A. Slade School of Fine Art, has illustrated 30 books which have been translated and published in seven countries. She has achieved major commissions in both mural and fine art painting.

Helping Children Learn About Domestic Abuse and Coercive Control

A Professional Guide

CATHERINE LAWLER AND ABIGAIL STERNE
ILLUSTRATED BY NICKY ARMSTRONG

Routledge
Taylor & Francis Group

LONDON AND NEW YORK

First published 2021
by Routledge
2 Park Square, Milton Park, Abingdon, Oxon OX14 4RN

and by Routledge
52 Vanderbilt Avenue, New York, NY 10017

Routledge is an imprint of the Taylor & Francis Group, an informa business

British Library Cataloguing-in-Publication Data
A catalogue record for this book is available from the British Library

Library of Congress Cataloging-in-Publication Data
Names: Lawler, Catherine, author. | Sterne, Abigail, author. | Lawler, Catherine. Floss and the boss.
Title: Helping children learn about domestic abuse and coercive control : a professional guide / Catherine
    Lawler and Abigail Sterne ; illustrated by Nicky Armstrong.
Description: Abingdon, Oxon ; New York, NY : Routledge, 2020. | Includes bibliographical references.
Identifiers: LCCN 2020008371 (print) | LCCN 2020008372 (ebook) | ISBN 9780367510817 (paperback) |
    ISBN 9781003052364 (ebook)
Subjects: LCSH: Family violence. | Victims of family violence--Services for. | Victims of family
    violence--Counseling of. | Child welfare.
Classification: LCC HV6626 .L388 2020 (print) | LCC HV6626 (ebook) | DDC 362.82/92071--dc23
LC record available at https://lccn.loc.gov/2020008371
LC ebook record available at https://lccn.loc.gov/2020008372

ISBN: 978-0-367-51081-7 (pbk)
ISBN: 978-1-003-05236-4 (ebk)

Typeset in Antitled
by Servis Filmsetting Ltd, Stockport, Cheshire

This book is dedicated to my mum Carole, who was unfalteringly kind and stronger than she ever gave herself credit for. Also to my big fluffy childhood dog Sheba, who was a bundle of love and companionship in dark times.

When you are a survivor of coercive control and domestic abuse, it's like being in a club, a club to which you don't necessarily want to belong, but with whose members you identify and want to help. I hope this book will help the amazing grown-ups that support children and their families. More importantly, that it supports the brave little people who live with and live through the insidious terror that is domestic abuse.

Catherine

Contents

Foreword

Floss and the Boss is a pathbreaking book.

Children living with coercive control experience multiple different forms of abuse from the perpetrator. Previous children's books have tended to focus on one of these, physical violence. This book is the first to widen the focus and engage with the many aspects of coercive control that children experience.

Coercive control is a severe form of domestic abuse. How it impacts children is an issue requiring urgent recognition and addressing, because the children who experience it are particularly in need of attention and support. They deserve to be considered both as the children of victims/survivors, and as victims/survivors in their own right.

The book is beautifully illustrated and carries a simple and extremely powerful story. The story itself is pitched just right for young children to engage with on a number of different levels. It would be useful for all children, regardless of whether they themselves are experiencing coercive control. The resources that accompany it are absolutely excellent for supporting professionals to use the book with children.

With its vitally important message and engaging story, *Floss and the Boss* is an essential resource.

Dr Emma Katz, Ph.D.
Senior Lecturer in Childhood and Youth,
Liverpool Hope University, UK

Acknowledgements

Our thanks are due to:

The Y6 children of Crab Lane Primary School, Manchester for such well-written and helpful book
   reviews
The Y1 children of Werneth Primary School, Oldham for their thoughtful feedback
Laura Davidge, David Dodd and Tracy Shackleton, Crab Lane Primary School
Katie Malley and Zoe Cunliffe, Werneth Primary School
Dr Lynda Dodd, Dr Sarah McIntosh and Corinne Abisgold, OneEducation, Manchester
Len Grant

Introduction

This book aims to help professionals talk to primary school children about domestic abuse, coercive control and safety planning. It is for use by teachers, learning mentors, social care staff, counsellors and therapists. It can be used with individuals and small groups but also with whole classes, as a means of addressing a sensitive issue. The story focuses on some of the typical, lived experiences of coercive control from a child's perspective, in this case when a step-parent moves in with the family. It portrays a difficult family situation, with which some children will identify. It highlights a range of detrimental effects on the child.

Domestic abuse and coercive control are widely regarded to be one of the most common and pernicious adverse childhood experiences (ACEs). Victims report that the non-physical elements often cause them the most pain and trauma and this story focuses on these. Also, Stark (2007) states that coercive control is gendered, 'in that it relies for its impact on women's vulnerability *as women* due to sexual inequality'.

The *Floss and the Boss* story should help some children feel that their experiences of living with coercive control are validated and can be understood; that they are not alone; that this is not unique to their family. It illustrates that there are grown-ups in their world who can help.

The book should place professionals in a position to have important conversations with children about what to do if something at home does not feel right and if they are feeling fearful and worried about themselves or a parent/carer. It provides a vehicle for talking to children about staying safe and about emotional wellbeing. Recent research highlights the importance of talking directly to children about their capacity to cope in situations of domestic violence and abuse to help them develop coping strategies (Callaghan et al., 2015).

Professionals are consequently helped to respond to children's needs in a number of ways, including:

- safeguarding them, through following appropriate procedures
- involving them in safety planning (Kress et al., 2012)
- providing key adult support, empathy and a listening ear
- engaging and supporting mothers; signposting them to specialist services
- providing appropriate nurturing, enriching and soothing experiences.

1. The characters

Floss

Floss represents a child whose home environment becomes one of coercive control and domestic abuse. Her story portrays the typical thoughts, feelings, reactions and behaviours of a young child who is stressed and scared. The story shows her route to accessing support from a key, empathetic, emotionally available, adult in school, who may also support her mother and alert safeguarding services.

Floss's Mum

Mum represents a parent who becomes a victim of coercive control and domestic abuse. Her story illustrates the impact on parenting and on her sense of self.

Boss

Boss is a perpetrator of domestic abuse and coercive control; he represents a step-parent who moves into the family home. His actions and behaviour are typical tactics perpetrators use to coerce and control their partners and children. Floss and Mum become frightened of him.

Houdini

Houdini the hamster represents a friend or a family member who is gradually isolated from Floss and Mum.

Wagtail

Wagtail is the key adult in school who may have been informed about Floss's circumstances (e.g. through a referral or notification) or may just have picked up that something is wrong. Over time, Wagtail gains Floss's trust and encourages Floss to talk about what is worrying her.

Wagtail provides a listening ear, monitors Floss's wellbeing and provides therapeutic play activities. Wagtail also reaches out to Mum.

2. Page by page teacher/ mentor notes

p. 1   Floss represents a well-nurtured child; she and her mum are emotionally connected. Floss is much-loved and happy.

p. 2   Floss and Mum live comfortably and are part of their community. Floss enjoys school, has routines and structure; all foundations for a happy childhood.

p. 3   Houdini is a friend or a family member with whom Floss experiences joyfulness, playfulness, relaxation, fun and laughter.

p. 4   At bedtime, Floss has a cuddle, is relaxed and has a good sleep. She feels safe and secure.

p. 5   Mum's new partner Boss is introduced to Floss.

p. 6   Boss impresses and endears himself to both Mum and Floss.

p. 7   Boss is trying to integrate himself into different aspects of their lives.

p. 8   Very quickly, Boss moves into the family home, subtly begins to undermine Mum's authority and autonomy and takes charge.

p. 9   Soon, an environment of uncertainty and pervasive fear is created. Boss's controlling behaviour is intermittent and unpredictable and Mum would feel she always has to watch her step.
(This would create stress and anxiety in Floss who would feel worried, scared and confused; the uh-oh feeling).

p. 10   Boss attempts to create tension and distance between Floss and Mum. This is a typical manifestation of coercive control. Behaviours include:
- asserting male privilege by being rigid and making trivial demands; Boss has to eat first
- demanding obedience by using coercion and intimidation; Floss's play must not disturb him
- isolation from sources of support; no going out without Boss; keeping Houdini, the friend, at bay. Control of time, space and movement. Continual monitoring
- undermining Mum as a parent; an assault on the child–parent relationship; using the child to control the adult (forbidding the bedtime story).

p. 11   The nip represents physical aggression, a feature of coercive control. Floss is frightened and traumatised.

p. 12   Floss displays somatic responses to trauma, including:
      Feelings of intense anxiety.

p. 13   Tummy aches and headaches.

p. 14   Not wanting to eat, feeling sick.

p. 15   Difficulties sleeping, waking up because of nightmares.

p. 16   Floss displays separation anxiety. She resists going to school and would prefer to be with her mother, so that she can know that Mum is safe.

p. 17   In school, Floss is preoccupied with thoughts about her mother being hurt. She finds it hard to concentrate and engage with learning and play.

p. 18   She finds it difficult to stay calm, regulate her emotions and she may be in a high state of arousal. There are fall-outs: she may feel cross and may resist doing what she is told.

p. 19   Wagtail is a key adult; maybe a teacher, teaching assistant or mentor, who responds calmly and empathetically to Floss and is curious about the underlying reasons for the behaviour change.

p. 20   Floss is reluctant to speak, out of fear of the consequences of disclosing information to an adult. For traumatised children, words can be difficult to find.

p. 21   Over time, Wagtail develops a positive and trusting relationship. Wagtail is emotionally available and works hard to build rapport with Floss. Floss discloses information about the abuse at home. Wagtail acknowledges and validates Floss's lived experience.

p. 22   Wagtail contacts Mum to raise concerns and offer support. Wagtail also shares information with relevant people and agencies; this is likely to include a safeguarding lead. (Parents often find it difficult to talk to their children about domestic abuse and coercive control, including how it affects them).

p. 23   Wagtail engages Floss with fun, therapeutic activities. These are soothing and calming. Through a story, safety planning is done with Floss.

p. 24   Now Floss has a team of caring adults around her who are aware of her difficulties and responsive to her needs. This reduces her anxiety somewhat. Children often feel they are to blame for what is happening, so it is important to explore this with them.

Here is the opportunity for a child or a group of children to contribute their ideas about what they could do in Floss's situation, or maybe if someone they know is in Floss's situation. It can include discussion about safety planning (see Chapter 3).

About the ending ...

We have deliberately left an open ending. Some children and their parent escape abusive situations. Mum and Floss might have gone to a refuge. Yet the reality for many children, even where social care services have been involved and there is close family monitoring, is that they continue to live in environments where coercive control is omnipresent and there is the potential for further domestic abuse. Katz (2019) also outlines how in this context, some mother and child relationships can become strained and distant.

Children will benefit from having access to key adults (represented by Wagtail) who can help them express difficult feelings and fears. A key adult can also liaise with the mother and support communication about difficult issues between her and her child (see Chapter 3).

For some children and families, this can trigger multi-agency work, where safety planning and protective strategies can be agreed, implemented and monitored.

3. Discussions and activities for supporting children, safety planning and supporting mothers

Recent research highlights the importance of talking directly to children about their capacity to cope in situations of domestic abuse (Callaghan et al., 2015).

The Floss story creates opportunities for adults to do this by exploring fearful and anxious feelings related to home and family life. Children can be helped to use and experiment with language relating to feelings. It can support some children to make sense of how they are feeling and what they are thinking. More broadly, it should help *all* children explore the concept of fear, safety and what they and others can do if they do not feel safe or well looked after. The key underlying messages that should be conveyed to all children are that:

- their safety and wellbeing are important; adults should keep them safe
- their thoughts and feelings matter
- if they feel fearful, they should seek help
- there are adults outside the home who can be trusted
- such adults may be able to help them, even in a situation that seems very difficult
- they can be helped to enjoy school and have fun.

Key questions and discussion points about feelings

How does Floss show she is happy/sad/frightened/angry?

How does Floss's body show us she is feeling sad/scared/angry?

What is Floss's face telling us?

How do we know she is feeling cold and prickly?

Where in her body would she feel the uh-ohs? What would they feel like?

Who could she talk to about her difficult feelings?

Why might Floss think that the difficult things at home were her fault?

What helped Floss to feel safer and better?

Using the story to support children's thinking about safety in the home

The story can be used to talk to children, including quite young children, about physical and emotional safety and identify ways of keeping safe in the home. Questions might include:

- Where could Floss go to in her house if arguing and scary noises are happening?
  Floss might move away, for example, to another room.

- What could Floss do whilst she is in the other room?
  Encourage the children to think about things that can distract or comfort Floss.

- Who could Floss go to if she has uh-oh or wobbly feelings?
  Encourage children to identify who Floss might feel safe with or who may be helpful. Mum? Wagtail? Houdini? Who would they themselves go to? Be creative, for example make a safety map/ helpers' map.

- Who could children go to if they had these feelings?
  This is an opportunity to talk about other adults who might help; for example, family support workers, social workers, community police officers.

- If Floss has big feelings inside her head and body that don't feel good, what can help?
  Talk about fun activities, relaxation and mindfulness techniques.

- What could we say to make Floss feel cared about?
  It might be appropriate to explain that it is not a child's fault if the adults argue. It also enables children to provide kind words and positive affirmations to Floss.

Finally, after discussing the above, summarise what has been suggested. Go back to the start of the story and pull out the main themes i.e. Floss's safe place, who Floss's helpers are.

Using the story to create a safe space in the classroom or within a school

Increasingly, classrooms and schools have so-called 'safe-spaces' to which children can retreat when they are agitated. This can be helpful for children when school have received a notification about domestic abuse. Could you create a 'Floss Corner' in your classroom?

Therapeutic play and safety planning

Much research highlights the significance of positive interactions as potential buffers to the impact of childhood trauma. Castelino (2009) also outlines the importance of children having agency within their situations, of aiming to collaborate with children 'to access their imagination, knowledge, and resources in order to create a safer family environment for the child'.

Professionals who see a child very regularly, for example a teacher, teaching assistant, family support worker or learning mentor, are in prime position to offer practical and therapeutic support. Trusting relationships with familiar, key adults can be of great importance to children with a challenging home life. Adults close to the child can:

- nurture a vulnerable child, give them a boost, providing additional pastoral care
- listen to the child, help them with their thinking and understanding, take their views and ideas seriously
- provide therapeutic play activities
- monitor wellbeing and notice changes in mood
- liaise closely with the parent and refer on to other supporting agencies.

Many children affected by domestic abuse and coercive control have significant social, emotional, behavioural and learning needs. Some may be angry and disruptive. Others may dissociate, be withdrawn and internalise their feelings. Some may find it difficult to learn and play harmoniously with their friends. Anxiety about home events may distract from learning and play. Attendance and punctuality may be poor, or children may have missed out on periods of education.

Support and enrichment through therapeutic play

The importance of play to children's wellbeing is well documented. With therapeutic play, the child takes the lead. It is their special time with an adult and it should be a safe way to project their feelings. The child can work through their worries and develop their confidence to communicate. For some children, toys can be their words and play their conversation. Therapeutic play can help the adult understand how the child sees their world.

For key approaches within the context of domestic abuse and coercive control, think of the three Cs:

Containment: Create a safe space to help a child in a state of high arousal to regulate and feel calm; facilitate the expression of their feelings, some of which may be distressing and overwhelming

Consistency: Provide an 'always available' key adult, wherever possible, to be a safety anchor for the child. Within school, provide structure, predictability and reliability

Curiosity: Be inquisitive and show genuine interest in the child and their life. What is happening to make them behave the way they are doing?

The key adult role

Children living in homes with domestic abuse and coercive control may not have had the opportunity to internalise a sense of safety, security and trust in adults. Developing a trusting relationship with a supportive adult in school may take time, though a child may take the initiative and turn to an adult out of the blue.

Qualities of an effective key adult

Qualities in a key adult include an ability to be:

- calm, confident, empathetic and a good listener
- patient and persistent
- fun-loving
- reliable and consistent in their responses
- proactive; good at networking within and beyond school
- empathetic and trauma informed.

This role will work best when it is embedded in a positive school ethos. Effective supervision is essential. This means having time allocated with other professionals for case consultation. A key adult should feel supported and able to refer on, or signpost the parent, as appropriate.

Building a relationship, developing rapport

Kind, understanding, warm and empathetic relationships have great therapeutic impact. Vulnerable children will particularly benefit from adults who:

- can provide a sensitive response to separation anxiety
- are aware of a child's physical care needs; some children may arrive at school tired, hungry and thirsty; snacks and a drink are nurturing
- understand attachment and its relevance to children who need warmth and care from one or two key adults
- can nurture the child and communicate that they are unique and valued; can provide a secure base and a predictable routine; where possible the same room, same start time, same snack on offer
- can provide soothing sensory experiences; opportunities for peace, quiet and relaxation
- can encourage the child to recognise and express feelings
- can help the child explore the concept of safety.

Responding to a domestic abuse notification

Recent initiatives such as Operation Encompass, whereby schools receive notifications of very recent domestic abuse incidents, mean that increasingly, schools are being made aware that children may be arriving in a state of distress. It will be helpful for schools to have strategies to meet the needs of such children. The following therapeutic approaches should be particularly helpful to children who are distressed on arrival, or struggle to self-regulate during the day.

Approaches to helping children soothe and self-regulate

Containment; the 'calming corner'

Stressful home incidents can leave children overwhelmed and dysregulated, so provide a safe space for retreat; teach the child calming strategies and provide a calming kit. This may include a safe blanket or weighted blanket, sensory and soft toys and soothing music. Children may need help to communicate they need their safe space so pre-agree a word, gesture or provide an expression card.

Mindfulness activities can be helpful. Traumatised and frightened children are often in a heightened state of arousal and can perceive the simplest of situations as threatening. Mindfulness techniques can help minds and bodies to calm.

Butterfly hugs

The butterfly hug can soothe and focus children when they are experiencing strong emotions. The key adult can demonstrate to the child how to cross their arms, pat their back and be aware of their breathing. You can also count the pats, visualise a butterfly flapping its wings and describe the butterfly.

Breathing bubbles

Most children love bubbles. As well as providing mutual enjoyment, bubbles can enable children to control their breathing and relax.

After doing bubble popping, ask the child to blow only one big bubble. The adult teaches the child to take deep breaths from the stomach then slowly exhale.

With some children it may be possible to explain that if they become angry or anxious and breathe deeply in the same way, it should help them calm down rather than do angry actions.

Using technology for relaxation

Free apps such as *Chill Panda* and *Sesame Street Breathe* can help little brains and bodies calm down.

Sensory soothing toys/bags

With sensory toys such as playdoh, aroma dough, slime, fidget toys, the rhythmic movements can help anxious children calm down; joint activities help with rapport building.

Cuddle buddies

Cuddly toys can help children self-soothe and can also be used to help them think about the concept of safety:

- 'Where could teddy go if she did not feel safe?'
- 'What could teddy do if he did not feel safe?'
- 'How might teddy feel?'

The activities below can emphasise eye contact, touch, physical closeness, rhythmic movements and mutual enjoyment:

Singing/action rhymes

Ones that involve touch include Row the Boat, Round and Round the Garden, Rock-a Bye Baby.

Physical activities

Kicking a ball, jumping jacks, hopping, skipping, running, banging a drum, throwing bean bags and relaxation exercises; these can all help children calm down and will release endorphins that trigger positive feelings.

Art and craft activities

Painting, collage and card-making appeal to many children and provide opportunities for self-expression. Messy activities may be discouraged in homes where there is a high level of control.

Puppy love/pet power

Sometimes schools have pets. Stroking animals can be soothing for stressed or anxious children. They encourage playfulness and produce an automatic relaxation response.

Puppets, dolls house and small world toys and role play

These can help children express and explore feelings. Difficult situations can be acted out and the child can project their thoughts on to the puppets or toys. This can enable the adult to gain insight into the child's world. (Note that many children will play imaginatively and act out fantasies. Beware of placing adult interpretations on the child's observations or language).

Create a child's own relaxation backpack or calming case

An individual relaxation backpack/box can contain the resources the child chooses to help them feel calm, safe and regulated.

Safety planning with individuals

When it is known that children are living with domestic abuse and coercive control, safety planning is of paramount importance and will often be done in collaboration with the non-abusing parent and other agencies.

The *Floss and the Boss* story can be a helpful and non-threatening way to introduce a child to safety planning, initially by thinking about what Floss might do to stay safe; this might then lead to discussion about a child's own situation.

In the previous section, questions have been suggested to help a group of children think what Floss might do if there was an unsafe situation. When working one-to-one with a child, these might lead on to encouraging them to reflect on their own situation:

- Can you tell me/draw where you might go in your home? Draw yourself in your safe space, feeling safe.
- What could you do while you are there? What would you do? Could you hold your cuddly toy tight, talk to it, sing a song, breathe calm feelings you're your tummy?
- Where would you go to if you have uh-oh feelings or wobbly feelings? Draw the people you might go to.
- If you have big feelings inside your head and body that don't feel good, what can you do? (Talk about some of the relaxation techniques you have introduced.) What makes you feel better?

School trip

In order to further explore the concept of safety, the adult could take the child on a trip round school to look at its key safety features and why they are there. For example, the purpose of emergency exits or where to line up during a fire drill can be a springboard for discussions about safety in the home.

Finally, summarise the key issues: the safe space; people to go to; calming activities. It will be helpful to communicate what has been discussed and planned with the mother.

Other helpful books for young children

Where the Wild Things Are (M. Sendak (1963), Harper and Row)
A children's classic. Max has adventures when he is sent to bed with no meal and sails away to a land of monsters. The illustrations contain a wonderful range of facial expressions that could stimulate discussion about different feelings and their underlying causes.

Misery Moo (J. Willis and T. Ross (2003), Henry Holt)
About trust and relationships; how friendship can weather anything. Somebody feels miserable and someone else keeps trying to cheer them up. This is relevant to how a child living with domestic abuse might feel; for example, Christmas being difficult. Children end up laughing.

Hands Are Not for Hitting (M. Agassi (2002), Free Spirit)

Words Are Not for Hurting (E. Verdick (2004), Free Spirit)
These books describe positive and negative uses of our hands, feet and of language.

The Huge Bag of Worries (V. Ironside and F. Rodgers (1996), Hodder Wayland)
A delightful story which can promote discussion on fears, insecurity and worries for young children, encouraging children to find someone who will listen to them. The child feels much better when she has shared her worries with an adult.

How Are You Feeling Today Baby Bear? (J. Evans (2014), Jessica Kingsley)
This sensitive story book is written to help children who have lived with abuse at home, to begin to explore and name their feelings.

Key adults supporting mothers

Domestic abuse has a detrimental impact on parenting. It can deprive mothers of the authority, confidence, physical and emotional strength to parent effectively. It can render a mother emotionally unavailable and make it difficult for her to play and interact positively with her children and put a strain on her relationships with her children. She may also find it difficult to impose behaviour boundaries. A mother may need help, but may feel so low and powerless that she does not seek it; the onus may therefore need to be on professionals to reach out to her. Key adults have an important role in getting to know and supporting the abused parent.

Supporting mothers can be fundamental to supporting children; Katz (2019) cites numerous studies that identify that warm, attuned, sensitive and responsive parenting from mothers tends to increase children's resilience and reduce the severity of the negative impacts that they experience. However, fear of repercussions from a partner can make it very difficult for some mothers to be open and express concerns or feelings. Staff should not interpret an apparent reluctance to engage as not caring, and labels such as 'hard to reach' can be unhelpful. The challenge is to build a trusting relationship and facilitate opportunities to talk.

Schools are ideally placed to reach out to mothers in need of help. Mothers visit regularly, often without their partner. Drop-off and pick-up times may be a mother's best or only opportunity for a chat with someone outside the family who has picked up that something is amiss. Developing a relationship may take time, commitment and sensitivity; trust is paramount. Bear in mind, some mothers may feel they need to keep authorities at a distance.

Some suggestions:

- Try to see the mother separately from her partner
- Be open; providing a listening ear
- Give her a private space and time to talk; it may help to ask open-ended, non-threatening questions, for example, 'How are things at home?'
- Help parents and young children build better relationships through play. Highlight the importance of this; demonstrate some of the therapeutic play activities
- It may be appropriate to signpost mothers to organisations for women experiencing domestic abuse (see helplines section) as well as specialist parenting programmes
- Provide information. Parents often wait in areas with noticeboards or leaflet racks. Posters and flyers can provide information about sources of support; they also give the message that the institution is aware of, and taking a stand on the issue.

Over time, a mother may be more open to talking about her situation, the pressures on her and her concerns. Some practitioners working to gain a better understanding of how a child is affected by coercive control may feel in a position to ask children and mothers about the constraints that are placed on their movements, their activities and who they can engage with inside and outside the home. Practitioners could also talk to children and mothers about whether there are things that they do, or refrain from doing, because of the reactions of perpetrators/fathers, and how this might be affecting children (Katz, 2016b).

Promoting, modelling and supporting positive play sessions with mothers and young children

Once a relationship of trust has been built with the mother, the key adult may be in a position to demonstrate and support play sessions with her and her child. This can be supportive of the mother and strengthen the parent-child relationship. By facilitating time and space with her child and modelling enjoyment of fun, shared play, such as the activities described above, staff can help re-establish the emotional availability of the mother.

In the longer term, professionals may be in a position to support mothers and children to talk to each other about domestic abuse. Research found that some children purposefully refrain from initiating discussions with their mother about domestic abuse, due to not wanting to upset or burden her (Mullender et al., 2002 and Humphreys et al., 2006). The following is a useful resource:

Talking to My Mum. A Picture Workbook for Workers, Mothers and Children Affected by Domestic Abuse (C. Humphreys et al. (2006) Jessica Kingsley).

This book is aimed at five- to eight-year-olds and features illustrated activities with animal characters. Themes include: exploration of a range of memories and feelings, including changes in the family's living arrangements, talking about their father or happy times with siblings and friends.

4. How children experience domestic abuse and coercive control

Definitions of domestic abuse and coercive and controlling behaviour

The UK Government defines domestic abuse as:

Any incident or pattern of incidents of controlling, coercive or threatening behaviour, violence or abuse between those aged 16 or over who are or have been intimate partners or family members regardless of gender or sexual orientation. This can encompass, but is not limited to, the following types of psychological, physical, sexual, financial and emotional abuse.

Controlling behaviour is:

a range of acts designed to make a person subordinate and/or dependent by isolating them from sources of support, exploiting their resources and capacities for personal gain, depriving them of the means needed for independence, resistance and escape and regulating their everyday behaviour.

Coercive behaviour is: an act or a pattern of acts of assault, threats, humiliation and intimidation or other abuse that is used to harm, punish, or frighten their victim (Home Office, 2015).

Professionals should note that coercive or controlling behaviour in an intimate or family relationship became a criminal offence in 2015, as part of the Serious Crime Act 2015.

A list of coercive and controlling behaviours from the Home Office (2015) includes:

- isolating a person from their friends and family
- depriving them of their basic needs
- monitoring their time
- monitoring a person via online communication tools or using spyware
- taking control over aspects of their everyday life, such as where they can go, who they can see, what to wear and when they can sleep
- depriving them of access to support services, such as specialist support or medical services

- repeatedly putting them down such as telling them they are worthless
- enforcing rules and activity which humiliate, degrade or dehumanise the victim
- financial abuse including control of finances, such as only allowing a person a punitive allowance
- threats to hurt or kill
- threats to a child
- criminal damage (such as destruction of household goods).

Professionals should note that the largest predictors of intimate partner homicide are emotionally abusive controlling relationships and victim instigated separation.

This diagram was produced to illustrate some of the various manifestations of power and control in domestic abuse:

DOMESTIC ABUSE INTERVENTION PROGRAMS
202 East Superior Street
Duluth, Minnesota 55802
218-722-2781
www.theduluthmodel.org

Victims of coercive control have described home life being like walking on eggshells; having to ask permission to do everyday things and living in constant fear of not being able to meet the abuser's demands. It involves extreme regulation of everyday life. Much recent research highlights how children are direct victims of coercive control.

We acknowledge that men are also victims of domestic abuse and that there may be many barriers for men within the help-seeking process. At the same time, coercive control is highly gendered; it involves fear and underlying threats of physical violence and is predominantly committed by men towards women.

Prevalence

Many children in nurseries and primary schools are exposed to domestic abuse and live with coercive and controlling behaviour. Some statistics:

- 12% of children under the age of 11 had experienced domestic abuse (Radford et al., 2011 in research for the NSPCC)
- 3.2% of under-11s reported exposure to domestic violence in the previous 12 months (Radford et al., 2011)
- 30% of children or young people had tried to intervene to stop abuse (SafeLives, 2017)
- 95% of children were often at home when the abuse took place (SafeLives, 2017)
- 74% were a direct witness to the abuse (SafeLives, 2017)
- 10% were injured as the result of the abuse of a parent (SafeLives, 2017)
- 18% were subject to neglect as a result of domestic abuse (SafeLives, 2017).

How living with domestic abuse and coercive and controlling behaviour affects children

For children living with domestic abuse and in a highly controlled environment, home is stressful and unpredictable and the family is a source of conflict. Some children feel always on guard, living in a state of almost constant fear and high arousal. This may include preoccupation with their mother's or their own safety.

Research conducted by Katz (2016a) into the harm inflicted by coercive control, describes how fathers/father-figures:

- controlled mothers' time and movements
- isolated mothers (and consequently isolated children) from sources of support
- produced family environments that narrowed mothers' and children's space for action.

Katz (2016a) states that these behaviours entrapped children (and their mothers) in constrained situations where children's access to resilience building and developmentally-helpful persons and activities was limited. The impacts of perpetrators/fathers preventing children from spending time with their mother, visiting grandparents or going to other children's houses may contribute to emotional and behavioural problems in children.

The following describe different ways in which a perpetrator may impose control on the family:

- micro-managing day-to-day activity and choices
- control of space, time and movement within the home, including the time the mother spends with her children and the rooms/space they can use; locking them in or out of the house; preventing the mother and children from leaving the house (Katz, 2016a)
- controlling and limiting their access to food. This can include imposing rules about what is eaten when, who eats first, who can touch the food in cupboards or in the fridge
- constraining children's self-expression and actions. Callaghan (2015) described how children adapted to accommodate violence and control: 'They learned to manage what they said and did to prevent themselves from being too visible, too loud, too noticeable to the abuser ...'
- unplugging technology (phones, internet, music) so children can't do their homework, contact friends or simply relax and escape (Katz, 2016a)
- disconnecting the electricity, limiting their ability to keep warm or wash, turn on lights, watch TV or use the internet (Katz, 2016a)
- controlling access to money; not allowing the partner to make decisions about financial transactions; making the partner account for what they are spending
- surveillance and monitoring. As well as making people account for where they are going and have been, perpetrators often use technology such as tracking apps so they can locate the whereabouts of family members at any time. They may insist on joint email addresses and social media accounts, having the same passwords. They may also track cars.

This type of surveillance can adversely affect children in that their mothers may have to stay at home to avoid further conflict (McLeod, 2018).

Citing research by McGee (2000) and Mullender et al. (2002), Harne (2011) states:

> Children and young people [describe] a catalogue of fathers' cruel and emotionally abusive behaviour towards them, such as destroying school work, school reports and toys, harming pets, not allowing children out of the house, not allowing them to speak to their mothers and not allowing friends to phone or come to the house. Some fathers are shown to deliberately emotionally abuse children and young people, insulting them and humiliating them in a similar way to their mothers.

Research suggests that 54% of children and young people are emotionally abused as a result of domestic abuse (SafeLives, 2017). Children living with coercive control are likely to experience significant anxiety and fear in their day-to-day lives. When considering the emotional impact of domestic abuse, the following figures are helpful:

- 23% of children feel or have felt they were to blame
- 41% were fearful of harm to themselves (SafeLives, 2017)
- 59% were fearful of harm to their parent (SafeLives, 2017).

For a child to live with the feeling that they are to blame for the abuse of one parent by the other can lead to toxic guilt and shame.

Swanston et al. (2014) describe children living with domestic abuse as 'miniature radar devices' who would attempt to predict the perpetrator's behaviour and response, despite this often being unpredictable. This was mirrored in the research of Callaghan et al. (2015). Children discussed how they would attempt to read the situation at home. One young person talked of attempting to read the perpetrator's mood and how he was likely to react to whatever she might say, however innocuous. She described always having to think ahead.

In summary, in *Working Together to Safeguard Children* (HM Government, 2018), the definition of emotional abuse is 'the persistent emotional maltreatment of a child such as to cause severe and persistent adverse effects on the child's emotional development'. For children living with domestic abuse and coercive and controlling behaviour, this includes:

- causing children frequently to feel frightened or in danger
- not giving children opportunities to express their views, deliberately silencing them
- placing limitations on their exploration and learning
- preventing children participating in normal social interactions
- hearing the ill-treatment of another
- serious bullying.

5. The impact of domestic abuse and coercive control on children's education

Exposure to domestic abuse and/or violence can have a serious, long lasting emotional and psychological impact on children. In some cases, a child may blame themselves for the abuse ...

Department for Education, 2019: 20

Living with domestic abuse and coercive control can prevent children from thriving in school. It causes distress, anxiety and affects their education in many ways. Each set of circumstances is unique, but different studies indicate that children living with severe or prolonged abuse are more likely to develop challenging behaviour and have significant social, emotional and mental health needs. They are more likely than others to find learning demands challenging.

In school, children may display:

- externalising behaviour; anger outbursts, aggression, hostility, aggression, oppositional behaviour
- internalising behaviour: shyness, withdrawn, passive behaviour, low mood, anxiety, low self-esteem.

Domestic abuse and coercive control can impact negatively on:

- early play and learning; ability to engage with play and learning activities
- early language development
- social interactions and social development
- feelings of wellbeing and good health
- attendance and punctuality.

Different factors will influence how and to what extent young children are affected. These include:

- the age and developmental level of the child
- the length of time they have been exposed to domestic abuse and coercive control
- the nature of abuse and levels of fear experienced. Children will worry about their mother's wellbeing and safety. Living in fear has a profound impact

- the impact of the abuse on the mother's ability to parent effectively
- the child's relationship with the perpetrator e.g. parent, step-parent, sibling.

It should also be noted that some children who live with domestic abuse and coercive control are high attainers; school can provide an escape. Yet in terms of emotional development, children are unlikely to emerge unscathed.

The psychological impact

Children who live in fear

Children living with domestic abuse and coercive control may live with high and sometimes unbearable levels of fear and insecurity. Some may feel under almost constant threat. They may be challenging when getting ready for school and use extreme delaying tactics such as running away or wetting themselves. They may be excessively clingy and stressed on arrival, finding it very difficult to separate from their mothers.

Some children may be so anxious as to feel ill (for example nervous tummy aches) during the day and worry about what will happen when they get home. Yet it is easy for the anxiety to go unrecognised in school. This type of emotional abuse can be a common and pernicious form of child abuse.

> Most of us can go home at the end of the day and relax and unwind; for these children, there's no let up. I've taken children home and they have sneaked in the house and they just don't want to be noticed.
>
> A family support worker

Children may fear:

- injury to their mother and themselves; disputes that might be happening while they are at school
- the stress and toll on their mother
- for the safety and wellbeing of other family members such as siblings, or their pets
- damage to their home or possessions
- the police arriving; the embarrassment of neighbours and friends hearing or seeing the violence
- family separation
- punishment and the consequences of telling someone.

Disrupted early attachments; confusion and distress for young children

Domestic abuse and coercive control can create multiple stressors for a mother, which can interfere with her ability to respond sensitively to her infant. She may suffer depression, be distracted from her child's needs and be emotionally drained. The more serious the levels of abuse are, the higher the likelihood of insecure attachment.

Infants are unlikely to make sense of the abuse and the highly controlled environment. For example, a mother may have to make efforts to have a quiet and 'non-crying' infant so a partner will not be provoked. No-one can explain what is happening and the mother's sense of helplessness can lead her to dissociate and act as if this is normal and there is nothing wrong.

The young child's thoughts and feelings about the experience become fragmented, disorganized and incomprehensible (McIntosh, 2002). Younger children generally do not have the ability to express their feelings verbally, so they communicate through their behaviour. By three years old, children exposed to domestic violence generally show heightened levels of distress and aggression. Young children experience great stress when they have no consistent or secure living environment.

Difficult feelings that young children may be carrying include:

A lack of trust and fear of authority figures; pressures to keep the abuse secret

Many children think domestic abuse must remain a family secret. Quite young children soon learn that it is not something that is openly discussed. They may fear making things worse and fear the repercussions of speaking to a professional. So children may avoid speaking about it or lie to disguise the perpetrator's behaviour. The circumstances of home life may leave children insecure and mistrustful of adults.

A child who has found adults to be unreliable or untrustworthy may have difficulties trusting professionals. They may already have observed that authority figures such as a controlling father, a social worker or the police can do sudden and drastic things. They may have already developed beliefs that people with authority are to be feared.

Feelings of responsibility, guilt, self-blame and confusion

Often, children feel that they are the underlying cause of the abuse. They will not understand the reasons for it so may assume they have done something wrong; maybe that their bad behaviour is driving a parent to it; that they have caused arguments or have made excessive demands for time and attention. They may therefore see themselves as the cause of conflict, so feel guilt and shame. These things are an enormous burden for children and likely to impact on self-esteem and wellbeing.

Children can feel they should try and stop physical aggression occurring and many do intervene both verbally or physically. In so doing, they can put themselves in danger.

The impact on personal, social and emotional development (PSED)

Let us now consider the three aspects of Personal, Social and Emotional Development (PSED) as set out by Early Years Matters (2019).

PSED is broken down into three aspects:

- Self-confidence and self-awareness
- Managing feelings and behaviour
- Making relationships

We can see how, living with coercive control can undermine a child's development in each aspect.

Self-confidence and self-awareness

This aspect is about how children come to develop confidence in who they are and what they can do and in expressing their own ideas. We know that ... all children need to have at least one person who is 'on their side' for them to really thrive. This helps the child feel valued and special and gives them a sense of self-worth. This in turn leads to them being confident with others and knowing when they need support from other people.

Early Years Matters, 2019

Research by Katz (2016) outlines how children living with coercive control may have, limited opportunities for self-determination. This can lead to them not feeling feel free to make choices, express ideas and develop a sense of independence and competence. In the classroom, we may see a child struggling to make choices about what they do, engage with the full range of play and learning activities, place themselves outside of their comfort zone, challenge themselves, take risks and ask for help.

Managing feelings and behaviour

This aspect is about how children can understand their own feelings and other people's feelings, and how they learn to manage their feelings without letting them spill out at every small annoyance they meet. It also links to how they learn and can follow simple rules which operate in different places such as home and a setting or a play area. Children need the support of adults to help them to understand these complex and often challenging areas.

Early Years Matters, 2019

Children who are frequently fearful and exposed to threat may have less control over their negative emotions and hence may display more distressed and disruptive behaviour (McLaughlin et al., 2014).

They can become agitated quickly and appear to over-react. An innocuous comment may touch a raw nerve, a seemingly minor incident can provoke stress or panic. Some children may respond to threatening or stressful situations by becoming aggressive and hostile; others may take flight and try and run out of a classroom. Children may be particularly sensitive to shouting, angry adult interactions and to physical contact. They are more likely than others to interpret their teachers and peers as having hostile intent. Severe behaviour outbursts usually indicate unbearable levels of tension.

Making relationships

This aspect is about how young children learn to get along with other children and with adults; how they can see something from somebody else's point of view and take that into account when they play and work with other children. It is also significant in developing friendships. To be able to do these things children need role models – adults who show them how to be with others; how to be kind and to understand why people behave in certain ways – such as saying sorry for hurting another person's feelings.

Early Years Matters, 2019

Domestic abuse and coercive control can adversely affect friendships and social interactions. Coercive control provides a negative model of how arguments are resolved. Children may observe that making threats and shouting are effective means of exerting control and getting their own way; in school and with friends, they may resort to similar tactics.

Some children may be clingy and possessive as there may be an underlying mistrust of others. They may cope with having limited control at home by being very controlling of their friends or with adults. They may like to be in charge and have difficulty working or playing to another's agenda. Some may find it difficult to maintain friendships.

> She's very possessive about her friends. Once she's formed a bond, she hates it to be threatened. With me too. If I have company, she won't leave me alone.
>
> A mother

Children who live in a stressful home environment may not want to invite their friends to play because of family volatility and unpredictability.

Speech, language and learning delay

Young children living with domestic abuse and coercive control are more likely to have delayed language and cognitive development. Reasons for this include:

- A home atmosphere of fear and unpredictability is not conducive to conversations, interactions, singing, language games and to a child imitating and trying out new sounds and words. As a coping strategy, young children may learn to keep quiet
- A mother who is anxious and depressed is much less likely to interact verbally and provide fun and stimulating play activities for her pre-school infant at a time that is crucial for language and cognitive development. A lack of environmental stimulation can lead to language deficits (McLaughlin et al., 2014)
- A high level of distress can make a child less able to engage with play activities and learning, concentrate and take in new information.

Attention and concentration difficulties; children on high alert

It can be difficult for children who are living in fear to concentrate in school. They can be in a continual state of high arousal. Teachers will be familiar with the child who cannot keep still, cannot sustain attention to an activity, who fiddles, rocks on their chair, turns around and gets out of their seat. Some children may behave impulsively: shouting out, poking others, lashing out, destroying their work.

Some children grow up feeling they always need to be on their guard; they may be 'hyper-vigilant' in school; continually scanning the class and distracted from their work.

> Children can blow at anything that triggers an emotional response. They are 'lighthouse children'. It's as if they put little beacons out and are waiting for the next thing.
>
> Primary learning mentor

Their preoccupation with their safety and that of their mothers can be another source of difficulties with concentration.

Some children may crave adult attention and behave so as to get it – negative attention being better than no attention. These children can be very wearing for staff; their behaviour impacts heavily on their learning and that of others.

Fatigue and sleep difficulties

Some children may be prevented from sleeping by arguments and fighting or be woken by them. Children who are anxious often take time to settle, may not sleep well and be woken by nightmares. Fatigue has an obvious impact on learning and behaviour.

Summary

Domestic abuse and coercive control have wide-ranging impacts on children's development and emotional wellbeing and this can affect their entire education and longer-term wellbeing. Children who live with high levels of anxiety and in fear for their safety and that of other family members are unlikely to achieve their potential or be content in school.

Domestic abuse and coercive control impact negatively on children's:

- emotional development
- behaviour
- ability to concentrate and learn effectively
- language and cognitive development
- friendships
- trust in adults
- attendance and punctuality
- attainments
- health and wellbeing.

Professionals may see young children who:

- find separation from their main caregiver distressing, so can be reluctant school attenders
- overly cling to adults
- have low confidence
- may appear passive, quiet, avoidant of others and reluctant to engage with play or social activities
- have not yet learned about sharing and turn-taking
- fear new people or situations
- show high levels of distress
- appear hyperactive and inclined to aggression towards adults and peers
- respond negatively to direction from adults
- are tired because of sleep disturbances and nightmares.

6. Helplines

Women's Aid is a charity that aims to end domestic violence/abuse against women and children. It provides a wide range of services and runs the national 24-hour, 7-days-a-week confidential domestic abuse helpline.
www.womensaid.org.uk/
0808 2000 247

Refuge supports women and children who experience all forms of violence and abuse, including domestic violence, sexual violence, female genital mutilation, forced marriage, so called honour-based violence, and human trafficking and modern slavery. Confidential domestic abuse helpline.
www.refuge.org.uk/get-help-now/
0808 2000 247

Men's Advice Line is a charity that offers help and support for male victims of domestic violence. They run a men's helpline.
www.mensadviceline.org.uk/
0808 901 0327

Galop run the national lesbian, gay, bisexual and trans domestic violence helpline.
www.galop.org.uk
0800 999 5428

Respect has a confidential helpline offering advice, information and support to help individuals to stop being violent and abusive to their partner.
www.respectphoneline.org.uk
0808 802 4040

Rape Crisis is an organisation that offers support and counselling for those affected by rape and sexual abuse.
www.rapecrisis.org.uk
0808 802 9999

National Association for People Abused in Childhood (NAPAC) offers support to adult survivors of all types of childhood abuse, including physical, sexual, emotional abuse or neglect.
https://napac.org.uk/
0808 801 0331

Shelter helps people with housing needs by providing expert advice and support; they also run a national helpline.

https://england.shelter.org.uk

0808 800 4444

NSPCC is the UKs leading children's charity, preventing abuse and helping those affected to recover.

www.nspcc.org.uk/

0808 800 5000

Dogs Trust is the largest dog welfare charity in the UK.

www.dogstrust.org.uk/

0207 837 0006

RSPCA is the largest animal welfare charity operating in England and Wales. 24-hour cruelty line to report cruelty, neglect or an animal in distress.

www.rspca.org.uk/

0300 1234 999

Bibliography

Callaghan, J.E., Alexander, J.H., Sixsmith, J., Fellin, L.C. (2015) 'Beyond "Witnessing": Children's Experiences of Coercive Control in Domestic Violence and Abuse', *Journal of Interpersonal Violence*, 33(10), pp. 1551–1581. DOI: 10.1177/0886260515618946

Castelino, T. (2009) 'Making Children's Safety and Wellbeing Matter', *Australian Social Work*, 62(1), 61–73. DOI: 10.1080/03124070802430726

Department for Education (2019) *Keeping Children Safe in Education. Statutory Guidance for Schools and Colleges*. London: Department for Education. Available online: https://assets.publishing.service.gov.uk/government/uploads/system/uploads/attachment_data/file/836144/Keeping_children_safe_in_education_part_1_2019.pdf

Early Years Matters (2019) *Personal, Social and Emotional Development*. Available online: www.earlyyearsmatters.co.uk/our-services/school-and-nursery-improvement-partner/psed/

Harne, L. (2011) *Violent Fathering and the Risks to Children: The Need for Change*. Bristol: The Policy Press. Available online: https://policy.bristoluniversitypress.co.uk/violent-fathering-and-the-risks-to-children

HM Government (2018) *Working Together to Safeguard Children: A Guide to Inter-agency Working to Safeguard and Promote the Welfare of Children*. London: Department for Education. Available online: https://assets.publishing.service.gov.uk/government/uploads/system/uploads/attachment_data/file/729914/Working_Together_to_Safeguard_Children-2018.pdf

Home Office (2015) *Controlling or Coercive Behaviour in an Intimate or Family Relationship: Statutory Guidance Framework*. London: Home Office. Available online: www.gov.uk/government/publications/statutory-guidance-framework-controlling-or-coercive-behaviour-in-an-intimate-or-family-relationship

Humphreys, C., Mullander, A., Thiara, R., Skamballis, A. (2006) '"Talking to My Mum": Developing Communication Between Mothers and Children in the Aftermath of Domestic Violence', *Journal of Social Work*, 6(1), pp. 53–63. Available online: https://doi.org/10.1177/1468017306062223

Katz, E. (2016a) *Coercive Control-based Domestic Abuse: Impacts on Mothers and Children*. London: Presentation, AVA (Against Violence and Abuse) training seminar, 28 January. Available online: https://avaproject.org.uk/wp-content/uploads/2016/03/Emma-Katz-2016.pdf

Katz, E. (2016b) 'Beyond the Physical Incident Model: How Children Living with Domestic Violence are Harmed By and Resist Regimes of Coercive Control', *Child Abuse Review*, 25(1), pp. 46–59.

Katz, E. (2019) 'Coercive Control, Domestic Violence, and a Five-Factor Framework: Five Factors That Influence Closeness, Distance, and Strain in Mother–Child Relationships', *Violence Against Women*, 25(15), pp. 1829–1853. Available online https://doi.org/10.1177/1077801218824998

Kress, V. E., Adamson, N. A., Paylo, M. J., DeMarco, C., & Bradley, N. (2012). 'The Use of Safety Plans With Children and Adolescents Living in Violent Families', *The Family Journal*, 20(3), pp. 249–255.

McGee, C. (2000) *Childhood Experiences of Domestic Violence*. London: Jessica Kingsley Publishers.

McIntosh, J. (2002) 'Thought in the Face of Violence: A Child's Need', *Child Abuse & Neglect*, pp. 229–241. Available online: http://search.proquest.com/docview/230157740/

McLaughlin, K.A., Sheridan, M.A. and Lambert, H.K. (2014) 'Childhood Adversity and Neural Development: Deprivation and Threat as Distinct Dimensions of Early Experience', *Neuroscience & Biobehavioral Reviews*, 47, pp. 578–591. Available online: www.sciencedirect.com/science/article/pii/S0149763414002620

McLeod, D. (2018) *Coercive Control: Impacts on Children and Young People in the Family Environment*. Available online: https://www.norfolksafeguardingadultsboard.info/assets/DOMESTIC-ABUSE/RiP-CoerciveControlImpactsonChildrenLitReview3.pdf

Mill, J. and Church, D. (2006) *Safe Learning: How to Support the Educational Needs of Children and Young People Affected by Domestic Violence*. London: Save the Children and Bristol: Women's Aid Available online: https://www.eani.org.uk/sites/default/files/2018-11/cpsss_safe_learning_how_to_support_educational_needs_of_children_affected_by_domestic_violence.pdf

Mullender, A., Hague, G., Imam, U., Kelly, L., Malos, E. and Regan, L. (2002) *Children's Perspectives on Domestic Violence*. London: Sage.

Radford, L., Corral, S., Bradley, C., Fisher, H., Bassett, C., Howat, N. and Collishaw, S. (2011) *Child Abuse and Neglect in the UK today*. London: NSPCC. Available online: https://learning.nspcc.org.uk/media/1042/child-abuse-neglect-uk-today-researchreport.pdf

SafeLives (2017) *Children's Insights National Dataset 2014–17: Specialist Children's Domestic Abuse Services*. Bristol: SafeLives. Available online: http://safelives.org.uk/sites/default/files/resources/Children%27s%20Insights%20dataset%202014-17%20v2.pdf

Stark, E. (2007) *Coercive Control: The Entrapment of Women in Personal Life*. Oxford: Oxford University Press.

Swanston, J., Bowyer, L. and Vetere, A. (2014) 'Towards a Richer Understanding of School-age Children's Experiences of Domestic Violence: The Voices of Children and Their Mothers', *Clinical Child Psychology and Psychiatry* 19(2) 184–201. Available online: https://journals.sagepub.com/doi/abs/10.1177/1359104513485082